ENERGY SOURCES

Water Power

by Tracy Vonder Brink

A Crabtree Crown Book

CRABTREE
Publishing Company
www.crabtreebooks.com

School-to-Home Support for Caregivers and Teachers

This appealing book is designed to teach students about core subject areas. Students will build upon what they already know about the subject, and engage in topics that they want to learn more about. Here are a few guiding questions to help readers build their comprehension skills. Possible answers appear here in red.

Before Reading:

What do I know about water power?

- *I know water moves in rivers.*
- *I know dams hold water back.*

What do I want to learn about this topic?

- *I want to know how water power makes electricity.*
- *I want to learn how dams work.*

During Reading:

I'm curious to know...

- *I'm curious to know how electricity created by water power goes to a building.*
- *I'm curious to know if oceans are part of water power.*

How is this like something I already know?

- *I know buildings have electricity.*
- *I know oceans have a lot of water.*

After Reading:

What was the author trying to teach me?

- *The author was trying to teach me what water power is.*
- *The author was trying to teach me how water power can replace fossil fuels.*

How did the photographs and captions help me understand more?

- *The photographs helped me understand how water power works.*
- *The captions gave me extra information.*

Table of Contents

Chapter 1: Energy and Fuel

We need energy for everything we do. Energy heats our homes. Our bodies use it to live. It fuels our cars. But what is energy?

Energy is the ability to do work or to make something happen. Energy is everywhere. It comes in different forms. Heat, light, and sound are all forms of energy. The lights in your home use electrical energy.

In science, work is energy moving from one object to another. Your feet pushing against your bike's pedals are doing work that makes the bike move.

Transforming Energy

Energy can be transformed, or changed, from one form to another. Energy changes forms when it is used to make something happen. Wood has energy locked inside it. Burning the wood changes its energy into heat and light.

Heat and light are two forms of energy.

A fuel is something that is changed in some way to produce energy. Wood is a fuel because burning it releases heat and light. Food is fuel for your body. Your body breaks down what you eat and uses it as energy.

Fossil Fuels

Fossil fuels are nonrenewable energy sources. Nonrenewable means they cannot be replaced.

We use fuels to make heat and power. Coal, oil, and natural gas are fuels. They are burned to release their energy. They all come from underneath the ground and they formed over millions of years. These types of fuels are called fossil fuels. If we use them up, they cannot be replaced.

Climate Change

Fossil fuels give off **carbon dioxide** when they are burned. Carbon dioxide collects in a layer around Earth. This layer traps heat and warms the planet. As Earth becomes warmer, its **climate** changes. We need energy sources that will not run out and that will not change the climate. We need **alternative** sources of energy. One such source is water power.

Climate change harms people and animals. Impacts of climate change include higher temperatures and changes in rainfall. This can lead to wildfires and less water for crops. These changes affect where people and animals live and the food that they eat.

Chapter 2: Where Does Water Come From?

The water cycle is the movement of water in, on, and above Earth. All water is part of this cycle. A cycle is a set of steps that repeat. When a cycle reaches the last step, it starts over.

The Water Cycle

When the heat of the Sun causes water vapor to be released from bodies of water, it is called evaporation. When plants release water vapor, it is called transpiration.

Sunlight heats oceans, lakes, and other places that hold water. The heat turns liquid water into water **vapor**. Plants also release water vapor. The warm vapor rises to the atmosphere, or the air that surrounds Earth.

The warm water vapor rises up through the atmosphere. The cool air of the atmosphere causes the water vapor to turn back into liquid water, creating clouds. When a cloud fills up with enough liquid water, it falls as rain or snow. Then the cycle begins again.

Rain becomes snow if the air temperature in the clouds and all the way to the ground is below freezing.

Chapter 3: Capturing Water Energy

Energy in motion is called kinetic energy. Ocean waves or a flowing river have kinetic energy. The faster and stronger the water moves, the more energy it has. We use the water's kinetic energy.

Waterwheels

A Roman engineer was among the first to invent a waterwheel. He built one about 6,000 years ago.

The idea of water power moving machines is still used in today's hydroelectric dams.

A waterwheel is a machine turned by water. It changes the water's kinetic energy into **rotational** energy. Waterwheels were first used thousands of years ago all over the world.

Waterwheels need a source of flowing water. They have paddles attached to the wheel. The water pours over the paddles and pushes the wheel forward. The water's force turns the wheel.

Water Mills

A water mill uses a waterwheel to grind grain. The waterwheel is attached to rods and wheels inside the mill. When the water pours over the waterwheel, it moves. It turns the rods and wheels. The wheels grind the grain.

Chapter 4: Changing Water to Power

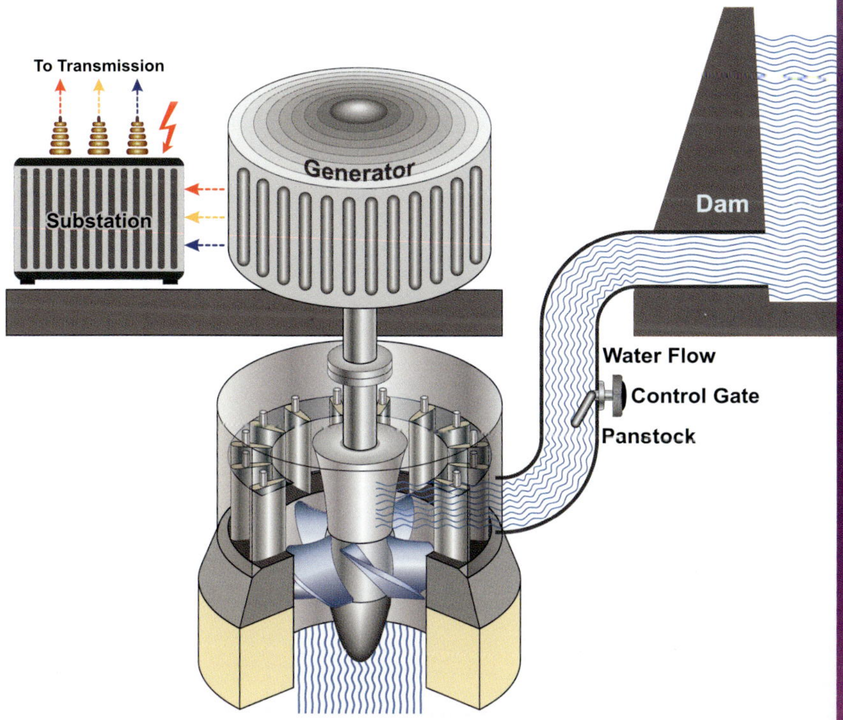

How do we use water to make electricity? Water flows through pipes in a **hydroelectric** power plant. The water pushes against the blades of a machine called a turbine. A drive shaft inside the turbine connects to a generator. As water flows over the blades, they spin and turn the drive shaft. Then the drive shaft turns the generator. The generator produces electricity.

A generator is a machine that turns motion into electricity.

Storage System Power Plant

China's Three Gorges Dam is one of the largest dams in the world. In 2020, it set a world record for most power produced by a hydroelectric dam.

A storage system hydroelectric power plant uses a dam to control a river's water. The dam stops the river's flow and creates a lake behind it. The dam can be opened to release water. Some flows into pipes connected to generators.

China's Three Gorges Dam is so big that it can be seen from space.

Pumped Storage Power Plant

A pumped storage power plant uses the water behind a dam like a battery. When the need for electricity is low, pumps move water into a higher **reservoir**. The water is released when more electricity is needed.

Run-of-River Power Plant

A run-of-river system uses a river's natural flow. A **canal** connects to the main river. Part of the river runs through the canal and into a turbine.

The canal is dug and connected to a river to make part of the river flow through it.

Ocean Power

Ocean waves and tides have kinetic energy. It might be possible to place turbines where ocean water flows in and out, but scientists are still studying this idea.

High and low tides could turn underwater turbines to create electricity.

Chapter 5: Powering a City

Electricity in a power grid may come from both nonrenewable and alternative energy sources.

The electricity generated by hydroelectric power plants travels through power lines to a **substation**. The substation changes the electricity into a form that can be sent to a **power grid**. All sources of electricity feed into the same power grids.

Electrical power may flow through several different substations before it reaches a home or business.

Smaller substations carry the electricity to towns and cities. Power lines above or below the ground connect them. Electricity flows from the substation into homes, businesses, streetlights, and more.

Water Needed

Not all areas have rivers useful for hydroelectric power, and many of the best spots for a dam have already been used. Rivers also have less water in times of **drought**. Less water means less electricity. In 2021, the United States produced 14 percent less electricity from water power after a record-breaking heat wave.

Cost to Build

Many of the dams in the United States are old. Repairing and improving them will cost billions of dollars.

Hydroelectric power plants are expensive, and building one takes a long time. In fact, water power is the most expensive form of alternative energy to build. China's Three Gorges Dam cost more than 28 billion dollars and took nearly 20 years to finish.

Harm to Animals and People

Dams block and change the way a river flows. Fish have a harder time finding food and laying their eggs. Turbines kill fish that swim through them.

Hoover Dam blocks the Colorado River between Arizona and Nevada in the United States.

St. Thomas, Nevada, was emptied when Hoover Dam was built. The town's buildings now lie under Lake Mead.

People who live in the path of a new dam may be forced to leave. China moved more than one million people to build its biggest dam. The United States also moved people as it built dams from the 1920s to the 1970s. Whole towns were emptied and flooded.

Chapter 7: The Future of Water Power

Water costs nothing. It is a clean source of energy. A large hydroelectric power plant produces enough electricity to power millions of homes.

Water power is the most widely used alternative energy source in the world today. It produces about 20 percent of the world's electricity. Some countries plan new dams, but others are turning to less expensive and less harmful sources of alternative energy. Will water power continue to be used in the future?

Glossary

alternative (ahl-TUR-nuh-tive): Something that may be chosen instead of something else

canal (kuh-NAL): A long, narrow waterway built by people

carbon dioxide (CAR-bun dye-OX-ide): A gas that is produced when people or animals breathe out or when certain fuels are burned

climate (KLEYE-muht): The usual weather conditions of a particular place

drought (DROWT): A long period of time with little or no rain

hydroelectric (HEYE-dro-uh-LEK-trik): Electricity made by machines powered by water

power grid (PAU-ur GRID): A connected system for delivering electrical power from power plants to homes and businesses

reservoir (REH-zr-vwahr): A human-made lake used to store water

rotational (row-TAY-shuh-nuhl): The act of turning around a center

substation (SUHB-stay-shn): Equipment that makes electricity usable for people

vapor (VAY-pr): Particles of moisture suspended in air

Index

Comprehension Questions

1. How do we use water to make electricity?
   a. Machines pull electricity from water
   b. Water powers batteries in the ocean
   c. Water turns a generator that makes electricity
2. How does a dam make electricity?
   a. Machines pull electricity from the water
   b. Water released from the dam turns a generator
   c. Closing the dam builds more energy in the water
3. What is one of the challenges of water power?
   a. Hydroelectric power plants are expensive
   b. Hydroelectric power plants are noisy
   c. Water produces carbon dioxide
4. True or False: Nonrenewable energy sources can be replaced.
5. True or False: Water is a clean source of energy.

Comprehension questions answer key: 1. c 2. b 3. a 4. False 5. True

About the Author

Tracy Vonder Brink loves true stories and facts. She has written more than 20 books for kids and is a contributing editor for three children's science magazines. Tracy lives in Cincinnati, Ohio, with her husband, two daughters, and two rescue dogs.

CRABTREE
Publishing Company

Written by: Tracy Vonder Brink
Designed by: Jennifer Bowers
Series Development: James Earley
Proofreader: Melissa Boyce
Educational Consultant: Marie Lemke M.Ed.
Print Coordinator: Katherine Berti

Photographs: cover ©2017 TommyBrison/Shutterstock, ©R2D2/Shutterstock; p.4 ©2021 Lin Xiu Xiu/Shutterstock; p.5 ©2015 Africa Studio/Shutterstock; p.6 ©2020 Natalia Leinonen/Shutterstock; p.7 ©2016 Tatjana Baibakova/Shutterstock; p8. ©2020 Sunshine Seeds/Shutterstock; p.9 ©2009 Mark Smith/Shutterstock; p.10 ©ArtMari/Shutterstock; p.11 © 2015 martinho Smart/Shutterstock; p.12 ©2013 Dark Moon Pictures/Shutterstock; p.13 © 2017 FLX2/Shutterstock; p.14 ©2018 Milkovasa/Shutterstock; p.15 ©2021 Irene Fox/Shutterstock; p.16 ©2018 Paul Brady Photography/Shutterstock; p.17 ©Fouad A. Saad/Shutterstock; p.18 ©2019 isabel kendzior/Shutterstock; p.19 ©2014 A. Aleksandravicius/Shutterstock; p.20 ©2014 Dmitry Naumov/Shutterstock; p.21 ©2012 Alex Mit/Shutterstock; p.22-23 ©2017 Jenson/Shutterstock; p.24 ©2019 Piyaset/Shutterstock; p.25 ©2013 orin/Shutterstock; p.26 ©2015 LMspencer/Shutterstock; p.27 ©2014 Steve Lagreca/Shutterstock; p.28-29 ©2020 BORJA PD/Shutterstock

Library and Archives Canada Cataloguing in Publication

Available at the Library and Archives Canada

Library of Congress Cataloging-in-Publication Data

Available at the Library of Congress

Crabtree Publishing Company

www.crabtreebooks.com 1-800-387-7650

Published in the United States
Crabtree Publishing
347 Fifth Avenue
Suite 1402-145
New York, NY, 10016

Published in Canada
Crabtree Publishing
616 Welland Ave.
St. Catharines, ON
L2M 5V6

Printed in the U.S.A./072022/CG20220201